EXPLORING THE STATES

Kentucky

THE BLUEGRASS STATE

by Patrick Perish

BELLWETHER MEDIA • MINNEAPOLIS, MN

Note to Librarians, Teachers, and Parents:

Blastoff! Readers are carefully developed by literacy experts and combine standards-based content with developmentally appropriate text.

Level 1 provides the most support through repetition of high-frequency words, light text, predictable sentence patterns, and strong visual support.

Level 2 offers early readers a bit more challenge through varied simple sentences, increased text load, and less repetition of high-frequency words.

Level 3 advances early-fluent readers toward fluency through increased text and concept load, less reliance on visuals, longer sentences, and more literary language.

Level 4 builds reading stamina by providing more text per page, increased use of punctuation, greater variation in sentence patterns, and increasingly challenging vocabulary.

Level 5 encourages children to move from "learning to read" to "reading to learn" by providing even more text, varied writing styles, and less familiar topics.

Whichever book is right for your reader, Blastoff! Readers are the perfect books to build confidence and encourage a love of reading that will last a lifetime!

This edition first published in 2014 by Bellwether Media, Inc.

No part of this publication may be reproduced in whole or in part without written permission of the publisher. For information regarding permission, write to Bellwether Media, Inc., Attention: Permissions Department, 5357 Penn Avenue South, Minneapolis, MN 55419.

Library of Congress Cataloging-in-Publication Data

Perish, Patrick.
Kentucky / by Patrick Perish.
    pages cm. – (Blastoff! readers. Exploring the states)
Includes bibliographical references and index.
Summary: "Developed by literacy experts for students in grades three through seven, this book introduces young readers to the geography and culture of Kentucky"–Provided by publisher.
ISBN 978-1-62617-016-2 (hardcover : alk. paper)
1. Kentucky–Juvenile literature. I. Title.
F451.3.P47 2014
976.9–dc23
                                                                            2013005835

Printed in the United States of America, North Mankato, MN.

Table of Contents

Where Is Kentucky?

Did you know?
In the southwestern corner of Kentucky, the Mississippi River makes a loop called the Kentucky Bend. It cuts off the corner of Fulton County from the rest of the state.

Indiana

Louisville

Mississippi River

Illinois

Mammoth Cave

Missouri ←

Tennessee

The state of Kentucky is in the east-central United States. Rivers run along almost all of its borders. In the northeastern corner, the Big Sandy River separates Kentucky from West Virginia. It flows north into the Ohio River. Across the Ohio River are Kentucky's northern neighbors, Ohio, Indiana, and Illinois.

Ohio

Ohio River

Big Sandy River

Frankfort

★

● Lexington

Kentucky

West Virginia

Virginia

N
W E
S

The Ohio River twists its way
southwest before flowing into
the mighty Mississippi River. Across it to the west is
Missouri. To the south, Kentucky shares a long border
with Tennessee. Its southeastern neighbor is Virginia.
Frankfort, the capital, is in north-central Kentucky.

Early **Native** Americans were the first people to enter the lands of Kentucky. The famous explorer Daniel Boone was an expert on the Kentucky wilderness. He helped settle the area in the 1700s. During the **Civil War**, Kentucky was divided. Most of its soldiers fought for the North, but some fought for the South. The war even divided some families.

Did you know?
Fort Knox holds the U.S. Treasury's gold. Electric fences, mines, and Apache helicopters protect its underground vault!

Fort Knox

Kentucky Timeline!

1600s: French, Spanish, and English explorers travel through Kentucky.

1774: Kentucky's first permanent white settlement is founded.

1775: Daniel Boone helps build the Wilderness Road. It connects eastern Virginia to Kentucky.

1776: Kentucky becomes a county of Virginia. Virginians settle there.

1792: Kentucky becomes the fifteenth state.

1809: Abraham Lincoln is born in a log cabin near Hodgenville.

1861-1865: Many Civil War battles are fought on Kentucky soil.

1900: William Goebel is shot the day before he becomes the state governor. He dies a few days later.

1937: Gold is moved to the U.S. Treasury's vault at Fort Knox.

Daniel Boone

Abraham Lincoln

Civil War

The Land

Cumberland Falls

fun fact !

Cumberland Falls in southeast Kentucky is also called the "Niagara of the South." It is famous for its moonbow. This arch of colorful light is only seen during a full moon.

Eastern Kentucky is part of the Appalachian Mountains. The rugged land is broken up by **plateaus**, valleys, and mountain streams. **Hardwood forests** blanket the region. In the northern part of the state is the famous Bluegrass Region. Its rolling hills and meadows are perfect for farming and grazing.

Western Kentucky is hilly with scattered farms. Large supplies of coal define this area. Deep caves hide under gently rolling hills. Far west, the Mississippi River **floodplain** provides rich soil for farming.

Mammoth Cave

stalactite ➔

stalagmite ➔

Mammoth Cave stretches for 400 miles (644 kilometers) underneath central Kentucky. It is the longest cave system in the world. Some 4,000 years ago, Native Americans explored the cave and searched for gemstones. Their remains and tools were discovered in the 1800s. The **artifacts** had been preserved by the cave's dry air.

Mammoth Cave is a world of wonders. Huge **stalactites** drop down from the ceiling, and **stalagmites** rise from the floor. The cave's creatures have adapted to life without light. Eyeless fish swim in underground lakes. At night, bats and crickets fly out in search of food.

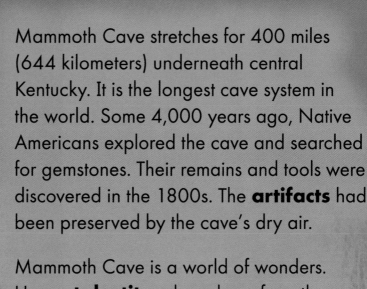

fun fact

Caves with entrances many miles away connect to Mammoth Cave. New tunnels are still being discovered in this underground world.

Wildlife

From the eastern mountains to the banks of the Mississippi, Kentucky is home to an abundance of wildlife. Raccoons and squirrels live in the ash and oak forests of the Appalachians. Bass, bluegills, and catfish swim the wide and twisting rivers.

Kentucky's **marshes** are important breeding grounds for herons and egrets. The meadows of the Bluegrass Region are home to goldenrods and other wildflowers. At dusk, thousands of bats pour out of Kentucky caves to feed. The whole state buzzes with life.

bluegill

big brown bat

raccoon

egret

Landmarks

There is a lot to see and do in the Bluegrass State! Horses are an important part of Kentucky culture. Visitors learn all about the state's history of horse racing at the Kentucky Horse Park in Lexington. In summer, daily parades showcase breeds from around the world.

Near Hodgenville, people can visit Abraham Lincoln's birthplace. A reconstructed cabin gives an idea of what life was like for early farmers. The Newport Aquarium stands along the Ohio River in the north. Visitors can check out rare shark rays and watch dive shows in underwater tunnels.

Abraham Lincoln's birthplace

Newport Aquarium

Louisville

Belle of Louisville

Louisville Slugger Museum and Factory

Louisville is a river city. In the 1800s, its bustling docks helped the city grow. Today, visitors can relive the early river days by taking a ride on the Belle of Louisville. This 100-year-old **steamboat** is the oldest of its kind to still carry passengers.

Did you know?
Every year, Louisville hosts the most popular horse race in the nation. The Kentucky Derby draws thousands of fans from the state and beyond.

Louisville has a special place in baseball history. It is the birthplace of the Louisville Slugger. This popular baseball bat was used by some of the sport's best players. Now the world's largest baseball bat stands outside the Louisville Slugger Museum and Factory. Visitors to the city stop here for the story behind the famous bat.

Working

In its early years, Kentucky was a farming state. Even today, farmers grow plenty of corn, soybeans, and hay. Most people in Kentucky work at banks, hospitals, and other **service jobs**. Others make cars, food products, and chemicals in the state's factories. Kentucky leads the nation in coal production. There is a giant coalfield on either side of the state.

The Bluegrass Region is known for producing some of the best horses in the nation. **Thoroughbreds** munch on the meadows of Kentucky bluegrass. Racehorses sell for thousands or even millions of dollars.

Where People Work in Kentucky

manufacturing
10%

farming and
natural resources
5%

government
15%

services
70%

Playing

Kentuckians love the outdoors. Fishing, hunting, and hiking are all popular activities. The Louisville Extreme Park is a huge concrete skate park in downtown Louisville. People show up every day to skateboard, roller skate, and bike.

Many Kentuckians enjoy playing and listening to music. In the 1940s, Kentucky native Bill Monroe and his Blue Grass Boys created a new sound. It featured lots of banjo, **mandolin**, and fiddle. The music style became known as **bluegrass**. Other popular styles of music in Kentucky are folk and country.

fun fact

The Louisville Extreme Park has a full-pipe that is 24 feet (7.3 meters) long! Expert skaters perform daring tricks inside the huge concrete tube.

Pegasus Pie

Ingredients:

Uncooked pie crust (premade or homemade)

1 cup sugar

4 tablespoons corn starch

1/2 cup butter, melted

2 eggs, beaten

1 cup walnuts, chopped

6 ounces semi-sweet chocolate chips

Directions:

1. Preheat oven to 350°F.

2. Combine sugar and corn starch in mixing bowl. Add melted butter and eggs. Stir in chocolate chips and walnuts. Pour mixture into uncooked pie crust.

3. Bake 30 to 40 minutes. Let cool for 10 to 20 minutes after removing from oven. Top with whipped cream or ice cream.

grits

burgoo

fun fact

"Whatever is on hand" means different things to different people. Adventurous eaters prepare burgoo with squirrel, raccoon, or opossum meat!

Early settlers in Kentucky relied on the vegetables they could grow, such as corn and potatoes. They raised pigs and sheep for meat. One favorite Kentuckian dish is burgoo. This stew is **traditionally** made from whatever is on hand. Beans, corn, and different meats all go in the pot.

Derby-Pie is a favorite local treat. True Derby-Pies are sold only from Kern's Kitchen. This chocolate and walnut pie is a Kern family recipe. A similar version called Pegasus Pie is made across the state. Kentucky cooking also features many Southern foods. Fried chicken, **grits**, and green beans are enjoyed throughout the state.

Festivals

fun fact !

Nearly 60 tons of fireworks are hauled in for the Kentucky Derby Festival. Its annual fireworks display is the largest in North America.

Kentucky festivals are all about food, music, and fun. The International Bar-B-Q Festival is held in Owensboro every spring. Judges pick a winning team of **barbecuing** champions. Lexington hosts the Festival of the Bluegrass every year. It is the oldest bluegrass festival in the state. People camp out and share their love of live bluegrass music.

Before the state's big horse race, Kentuckians celebrate with the Kentucky Derby Festival. They enjoy hot air balloons, parades, and a huge fireworks display. People across the state celebrate the end of summer with carnival rides and horse shows at the Kentucky State Fair.

The Kentucky Derby

Horse racing has a long history in Kentucky. Early settlers raced horses for fun. They soon discovered that Kentucky bluegrass helped horses become strong, fast racers. In 1875, Churchill Downs racetrack opened in Louisville. About 10,000 people came out to see Aristides win the first Kentucky Derby.

Since then, the Derby has become an important Kentucky tradition. When the horses step onto the field, everyone sings "My Old Kentucky Home." The 1.25-mile (2-kilometer) race has been called the most exciting two minutes in sports. Kentuckians gather together each year to share their state's proud tradition.

fun fact

In 1973, Secretariat set the Derby record that has stood for more than four decades. The horse won in just over 1 minute and 59 seconds.

Secretariat

Fast Facts About Kentucky

COMMONWEALTH OF KENTUCKY

UNITED WE STAND

DIVIDED WE FALL

Kentucky's Flag

Kentucky's flag features the state seal against a blue background. The seal shows an explorer dressed in buckskin embracing a statesman. Around this image is the state motto and the words "Commonwealth of Kentucky." A wreath of goldenrods lines the bottom of the seal.

State Flower
goldenrod

State Nickname:	The Bluegrass State
State Motto:	"United We Stand, Divided We Fall"
Year of Statehood:	1792
Capital City:	Frankfort
Other Major Cities:	Louisville, Lexington
Population:	4,339,367 (2010)
Area:	40,411 square miles (104,664 square kilometers); Kentucky is the 37th largest state.
Major Industries:	mining, manufacturing, farming, horse breeding
Natural Resources:	coal, farmland, timber, oil, natural gas
State Government:	100 representatives; 38 senators
Federal Government:	6 representatives; 2 senators
Electoral Votes:	8

State Bird
northern cardinal

State Animal
gray squirrel

Glossary

artifacts—items made long ago by humans; artifacts tell people today about people from the past.

barbecuing—cooking meat and other food over a rack on an open fire

bluegrass—a type of music that features banjos, mandolins, fiddles, and harmonious vocals

Civil War—a war between the northern (Union) and southern (Confederate) states that lasted from 1861 to 1865

floodplain—low land near a river; floodplains have rich soil that is good for growing plants.

grits—a dish of mashed corn boiled in milk or water

hardwood forests—forests of trees that lose their leaves in the fall

mandolin—a stringed musical instrument that is usually shaped like a teardrop

marshes—wetlands with grasses and plants

native—originally from a specific place

plateaus—areas of flat, raised land

service jobs—jobs that perform tasks for people or businesses

stalactites—icicle-shaped formations that hang from the ceilings of caves; stalactites are formed by mineral deposits.

stalagmites—cone-shaped formations that rise from the floors of caves; stalagmites are formed by mineral deposits.

steamboat—a boat powered by steam; steamboats were an important source of river transportation in the 1800s.

thoroughbreds—horses bred especially for racing

traditionally—according to customs, ideas, or beliefs that are handed down from one generation to the next

To Learn More

AT THE LIBRARY

Mitchell, Elizabeth. *Journey to the Bottomless Pit: The Story of Stephen Bishop and Mammoth Cave.* New York, N.Y.: Viking, 2004.

Sanford, William R. *Daniel Boone: Courageous Frontiersman.* Berkeley Heights, N.J.: Enslow Publishers, 2013.

Wiseman, Blaine. *Kentucky Derby.* New York, N.Y.: Weigl Publishing, 2011.

ON THE WEB

Learning more about Kentucky is as easy as 1, 2, 3.

1. Go to www.factsurfer.com.

2. Enter "Kentucky" into the search box.

3. Click the "Surf" button and you will see a list of related Web sites.

With factsurfer.com, finding more information is just a click away.

Index